A PLANET of HOPE

A PLANET
of HOPE

Robert Muller

AMITY HOUSE
AMITY, NEW YORK

Designed by Ernie Haim

Library of Congress
Catalog Card Number: 84-072842

ISBN: 0-916349-04-7

Published by Amity House Inc.
106, Newport Bridge Road
Warwick, N.Y. 10990

Printed and bound in the
United States of America

To

Dag Hammarskjöld
who inspired the world
with his *Markings*

CONTENTS

Foreword

It is a privilege to be the publisher of this book. But it is a greater privilege to call Robert Muller, its author, a friend. For Amity House is about friendships; those that are now being formed across the multiplicity of nations, races, cultures, disciplines and religions, and learning to be shared in a common caring for the earth and its peoples.

This is not a book about the planet. It is a planetary book. This is not a book about how to become a future planetary citizen. No. It is a book that suggests that hope is discovered in simply being what we already are, good humans, surely a people of God but yet who are nevertheless also a people of the earth.

Robert Muller is I believe a new man, for a new age. He is a hopeful, planetary person in a world inhabited by too many nay sayers, who perhaps are gifted with intelligence but who lack the energy of inspiration to make even their good ideas bear fruit. Jean Houston, the mind researcher and a spokeswoman for the emerging global consciousness calls Robert "the 21st Century man." By implication she affirms both that humans are being transformed and that there will be a 21st Century. For not withstanding the spectre of nuclear holocaust, to encounter a being like Robert is to feel the possibility of the truly human. He is a man who gives freely of a primal energy, an integrative wisdom, and a wondrous reverence for life that is surely the essence of human survival and ascent. More importantly this attitude is in touch with the wellsprings of those ultimately mysterious sources of life and happiness.

To present the pertinent biographical facts about Robert Muller, is to say little about him. Yes, he is Assistant Secretary General of the United Nations where he has co-ordinated the work of its thirty-two specialized agencies and world programs. Yes he is organizing the fortieth anniversary celebrations of its founding. Yes he was born in Alsace-Lorraine and was a member of the French Resistance during World War II. Yes, he and his wonderful wife Margarita (a former Chilean diplomat and delegate to the U.N.) have raised a fine family. Yes he has been with the U.N. since its inception. Yes, he was friend and advisor to Dag Hammarskjöld, U Thant and other U.N. leaders. But most importantly he is someone that one likes to be around; for one feels oneself elevated not only by his optimism, which is real, but by his awareness, that sees things precisely from a perspective of the whole world.

In this book Robert shares with his readers a collection of aphorisms. They are paradigms, axiomatic thoughts that have come to him in meditation, in the midst of work, when he least expected them. They are not just literary or intellectual pieces. They are deeper and more subtle. They have an oral quality. For Robert's strength is in relationships and thus he is not so much saying something, as speaking to someone.

Dag Hammerskjöld has said "God does not die on the day when we cease to believe in a personal deity, but we die on the day our lives cease to be illumined by a wonder beyond all reason". This is a book not only of reason but of faith. This is a book not only of belief but of the wonder of belief. For it participates in the very gift of life, of which it speaks. It is of that vision, without which we perish.

Richard Payne
President and Publisher,
Amity House

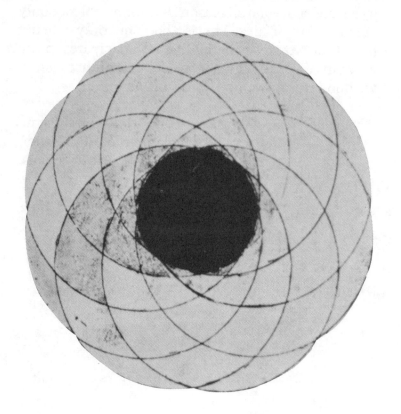

CHAPTER ONE

SPAN OF LIFE

These words uttered by Pablo Casals have
been a great guide for my life:

"The child must know that he is a miracle,
that since the beginning of the world there hasn't
  been
and until the end of the world
there will not be another child like him.
He is a unique thing,
from the beginning to the end of the world.
Now, that child acquires a responsibility:
'Yes, it is true, I am a miracle.
I am a miracle like a tree is a miracle,
like a flower is a miracle.
Now, if I am a miracle, can I do a bad thing?
I can't, because I am a miracle.'"

Someday,
population growth will be so slow
and life so precious
that people will thank God
for having been allowed to be born
and to live.

It is now well established that malnutrition, smoking, and alcohol during a mother's pregnancy affect the constitution and future of her baby. Is it not possible that her mental and psychological disposition may affect the baby too? We must, therefore, surround the child-bearing mother with all the love, consideration, and happiness possible. This is how we will get healthy, happy children. Peace requires a happy world. A happy world needs happy children. Happy children need happy mothers.

What is the greatest work of art on Earth?
A healthy, beautiful, well-educated, loving child.
Fathers and mothers are the greatest artists there
     can be on Earth.
A happy, loving family is more precious than any
     Rembrandt or Leonardo da Vinci painting.

It is the natural and perennial role of parents
to teach, to warn, to protect, to guide,
to help, to prepare, to "raise" their children,
Children, for their part,
have their own predispositions, nature, dreams, and
    likings.
The result will be a blending of all these,
of the past, the present, and the future.
And thus humanity proceeds on its evolutionary
    path,
epitomized and moulded
in each of the Earth's hundreds of millions of
    families.

Dear children and youth, remember always
that you are your parents' main contribution to
    evolution
and further human ascent;
you are their immortality;
you are their greatest work and joy
you will be their last thought and pride
at their moment of death.
You must think of the chain of life from which you
    come
as you will later think of the chain of life
    that comes from you.

One's family is his foremost church on Earth.
The most sacred acts are conducted in it:
love,
the gift of life,
care, protection, and education.

Children must early on learn
the value of respecting themselves and others.
Confucius was right when he advocated courtesy
    and respect
as the foundation of family and of society.

Someone said:
"We are educating children from the neck up."
How right that person was!
For what personal fulfillment, for what
    understanding,
for what kind of world are schools preparing
    children?
That is a question each educator should ask
    himself.

Life is divine. *Das Leben ist göttlich*.
I wish this exclamation of mine as a child
were translated in all languages
and displayed in every school on Earth.

Perhaps there are no barriers at all
between us and the universe,
except those created by ourselves and society.
As a child I could feel the immensity and divinity of
   life.
Then society came and created the barriers:
you must like this rather than that —
thus fragmenting and reducing my love.
A missing aspect of education:
teaching each student to love
the immensity and infinite variety of life.

In a school in Texas, the children are taught about their place in the universe in the simplest way: they are asked to fill out the following questions and to draw at the end a picture of their home. A child who has done this exercise will never forget it for the rest of his life:

WHERE ARE WE?

UNIVERSE_____

GALAXY _____

SYSTEM_____

PLANET_____

HEMISPHERE _____

CONTINENT _____

COUNTRY _____

STATE_____

CITY _____

STREET _____

NAME_____

You are truly a citizen of the Universe!

When I was a child, I spoke like a child.
   When I was an adult, I no longer spoke like a
   child.
When I became old and wise, I spoke again like a
   child.
   I wish I had always spoken like a child.

Asked, "What do you want to be when you are a
   grownup?"
a little girl answered: "To be alive."

Children should have the opportunity
   to learn from many people.
Everybody should be a grandfather,
   a grandmother,
an uncle, an aunt, a brother or a sister to a child.

Everything has been lived,
everything has been thought,
everything has been dreamt,
everything has been felt,
everything has been said;

but the great art of living is to live it all over again,
to think it again, to dream it again,
to feel it again,
to say it again *yourself*.

We are all fundamentally the same;
we are each unique and forever unrepeatable.
This is one of the beauties of the universe.

What is the most fascinating thing on Earth?
My own Being.
All external things are fascinating
only inasmuch as I see them as fascinating.
My own life,
my own functioning,
my own complexity,
my own capacity to love,
those are the most fascinating things on Earth:
I, a microcosm of the universe.

Life is a circle.
We are born,
we rise, we descend,
we return to Mother Earth, and we will be born
    again.
Like the stars in heaven,
like the vast universe,
like an atom, we are all circles.
There is no beginning or end.
There is no spontaneous generation from the void.
There is no death and emptiness.
We all come from somewhere and are going
    somewhere.

Every day is a new day.
But in reality there is no end to a day:
the sun slowly and unceasingly wakes up persons
    after persons
as the Earth turns around itself.
So it is with life:
we germinate under that sun, grow,
flower,
mature,
give birth,
and return to the Earth
in an incredible, unceasing cosmic journey.

Our lives resemble those of trees:
heavy winds and tempests make us stronger
and dig our roots deeper into the soil.
We must gain strength from every gust of adversity.

I am unique and fundamentally the same from birth
    to demise.
And yet every person I meet changes me a little,
as one particle changes another on its path.

We must allow the best to flower in each individual.
It would have been wrong to make Jesus into
a lawyer, an economist, or a scientist.

It is infinitely more important to live a full, happy
    life
than to occupy a glorified position.

Humanity is one living body made of human beings,
not of lifeless governments and institutions.
The latter are only the servants of life,
not life itself.

A human body constantly loses dead cells
and produces new ones.
It is the same with humanity.
People die, replaced by new cells,
our children,
and humanity continues to live as one body.
We must learn to be effective cells and parts of that
    body.

Every human person carries along with him a world
which is made of all that he has seen and loved.

In the middle of life,
all of a sudden one's ambitions, efforts, and beliefs
appear so confused, so obscure.
One feels lost, as though in a dark, thick forest.
The whole being longs for clarity, for open skies,
for the deeper truths of life.
Then begins the royal road of enlightenment and
    wisdom.
Then, too, the arrow of life points back again
to the dreams of one's youth.
During our adulthood there comes a time when we
    must be born again,
when we must find again the simplicity and
    resplendence of our childhood.

I regret that somewhere along my life modern society killed the two guardian angels I had when I was a child: on my left side I had a shining, white angel who told me what was good, and on my right side a dark, mournful angel who told me what was bad. They were my best friends and they were so useful. Then, as I grew up, I no longer believed in them and they vanished. When I grew older, I missed them so much that I called them back and they came immediately. So did my prayer to the good angel as it was taught to me by my mother:

"Angel of God, my guardian dear,
To whom God's love commits me here:
Ever this day be at my side
To light and guard, to rule and guide."

In the end, there will be only one question:
was my life worthwhile?
Was it a happy life?
And since my life is made up of many days,
I must answer that question every day:
Was it a happy day?
The highest art is the way we live each day.

When I was a child I wanted to touch the sky.
During all my life I have never ceased wanting to
touch the sky.
An artist is given a canvas and paint to make a work
of art.
We are given by God something infinitely more
precious:
living matter.
We must make a work of art of that living, divine,
cosmic matter.

Human beings are future oriented:
everyone mourns the fact that he will no longer be
alive in a hundred years;
but no one ever regrets the fact that he did not live a
hundred years ago.
Or could it be that we instinctively know
that the future will be better than the past,
despite our complaints to the contrary?

I have innumerable children:
my ideas and visions of how beautiful life on this
planet can be.

It would help us understand our life's objective if we were to say like St. Thérèse: "I will spend my heaven doing good on Earth" or if we decided to come back to Earth as a spirit to do what we really wanted to do.

Personally, I have decided to return as a spirit to needle heads of state to make peace and to administer this planet for the good and happiness of all.

Sometime, write down what you would choose for your epitaph. It can tell you a lot about who you are and how you relate to the universe and eternity.

No person is ever completely self-realized or
  fulfilled.
We learn and enrich ourselves until we die.
We gain new capacities and we lose old ones.
The art of living has no end.
It is too rich to be exhausted by a single life.

I want to take good care of myself in order to live very long and serve God and my planet well. To live long only for my personal purpose would be self-defeating: it is narrowness and inwardness which are the main killers of old age. When I am sitting in a bus or in a subway, I often close my eyes and say to myself: "I will live a hundred years and I will be immortal through my actions and writings." It may not be true, but it elevates me, makes me feel happy, and fills me with thoughts to achieve these two purposes.

There is no downward trend in life.
Advanced age is as precious as any other.
It is accumulated spirit, the culmination of a
   process,
an apotheosis of the miracle of life.
In so many civilizations the elders are the most
   respected and honored persons:
they are the slowly distilled essence of life.

Even and especially during old age, life can pursue its
upward course thanks to a passion, and that passion
can range over an immense gamut of reality: from the
infinitely large (e.g., God) to the infinitely small (e.g.,
a hobby). The object is unimportant—only the drive
for life, the will for life, the passion for what one is
doing counts.

How many wonderful sages there are among old
   people.
What life experience they represent
Old people should be our kings, our teachers, our
   masters.
Yet, we barely consult them.
To live is to search for truth.
They have lived longest and are therefore closest to
   the truth.

My physical body may be less efficient and less beautiful in old age. But God has given me a vast compensation; my mind is richer, my experience is wealthier, my soul is broader, my wisdom is at a peak. I am so happy with my old age that, contrary to Faust, I would not wish to return to my youthful ignorance.

Better an old man with an old heart that needs the help of a pacemaker than a young man without a heart.

I can look at my life companion and see her wrinkles, gray hair, and less voluptuous body, and desire a younger creature, or I can see in her all the happiness in the world, our younger years, our dreams, our efforts, our children, our present wisdom and serenity, the new being, mind, heart, and soul we form together.

The richest product of old age is wisdom and story telling.

Our life-long learning and search must have a
  reason.
Is it for ourselves?
Partly yes, but largely no, for we will die.
So it can only be to enrich humanity and its future
  journey.
My life makes sense therefore
only as part of the total flow of human life through
  time.
I am both part of the whole and part of a flow.

Once I was moved by an old centenarian French peasant woman being interviewed on television. Asked
about her views on death, she looked pensively to the
ground and murmured in a soft voice:

"The earth is calling me back. I can feel it.
The voice is getting louder every day.
The earth wants me back."

Only the Hunza tribe in Asia have the right concept of death: it happens at a very advanced age, at
night, during sleep. It is seldom preceded by sickness.
Death for them is the natural ending of a phase, a fall-
ing asleep, a peaceful, unnoticed transition to another
life.

To be able to say
on the last day of one's life:

    I loved to live
    I lived to love
    I laughed a lot
    I gave much love
    I left the world a little better than I found it
    I loved the world's great beauty
    I sang life and the universe
    I looked for the best in others
        I gave the best I had.

Thank you, O God, for this miracle of life.

Old age is the preparation for immortality.

I often feel as if my life were a lamp: a temporary container filled with light, a flow of energy, condensed and held together for a little while in a mysterious, marvelous living cosmos linked with the rest of the Earth and the heavens through material, touchable elements and immaterial, invisible elements. Someday the lamp will extinguish. The material elements will be reabsorbed by the Earth in its chains of life and energy. The immaterial elements will return to a universal soul to be reborn in other forms on this planet or elsewhere in the universe. We are cosmic matter come alive, partaking of the divine character of our Creator.

CHAPTER TWO

THE FOUR GREAT VIRTUES

GRATITUDE

Sometimes when I see nature, people, cars, airplanes, buildings, I stop walking and I say to myself: "What an incredible globe this is, turning at 1,666 kilometers per hour with so much life on it, with people standing on it, their heads pointing like antennae into all the directions of the universe, with leaves, plants, and algae avidly absorbing the sun's energy. And to think that we are the only planet of our sun, and perhaps of the entire universe, to possess life! How can we not stand in endless gratitude and awe before such a miracle?"

When I write early in the morning
it is with an immense feeling of joy and love.
To write can be a form of prayer,
a way of thanking God for the magnificent gift of
    life.

I sometimes sense God saying to humanity:
"You want to show me your gratitude?
Only be peaceful, be just and kind to each other
and grateful for every day of your life."

What an immense need there is—especially in the
rich countries—for deep gratitude!

Perhaps some day our world will be one of giving and
thanking instead of wanting and complaining.

The human being is such a wonderful, God-given
    instrument!
We can play on it the most moving and beautiful
    symphonies
or the saddest and most heartbreaking tragedies.
We must train ourselves to play on it joyfully,
    gratefully, and justly
in order to contribute to the overall beauty and
    happiness of our planet.

The most beautiful question a person can ask
    himself is:

"How can I be of service to Creation?"

What riches I can extract from the mere fact of being
    alive!
No wealth on Earth can ever match the worth of one
    single life.

Humanity fully depends on the sun and on this Earth, hence the need to respect our star and our planet, cherish them, and see them as sacred. And yet, we seem to have lost contact with them. We sleep and no longer pray when the sun rises. We live in cities of stone and cement. We watch television and hear radio instead of contemplating nature and listening to its beautiful sounds. We are wrong. We should make daily offerings to the sun and to the Earth and say with the psalmist: "This is a good day to live and to glorify God."

De Gaulle wanted to give France the best chance in the world.
Robert Schuman wanted to give Europe the best chance in the world.
I want to give the world the best chance in the world.

We must open ourselves to every potential,
to everything we can be,
to the vast world out there,
to the heavens, to God, and to eternity.
To be the vastest, the longest, the greatest,
the fullest living entity in the universe,
serenely and gratefully, that should be our purpose.

In the end, it is all a question of joyful surrender to the greatness of Creation and God.

HAPPINESS

What is the objective of life? To live fully one's life and to absorb with passion the universe around us while we are conscious of it. Happiness, *joie de vivre* are the oxygen of life. I sometimes feel that God is silently asking me: "Are you happy?" And when I say yes, He answers: "Then I rejoice at having created you."

We are rewarded with joys and happiness for the way we live our lives. This is how nature and God recompense us. Joy and happiness are therefore important yardsticks of our life-performance. To dwell with the subject of happiness is to seek the real purpose of our life.

You do not have to go very far to find happiness.
You can find it wherever you are.

Each morning when I awake,
I experience the extreme happiness of being alive.
Each day is a resurrection, a new birth.

To live happily, live hidden.
Be an extension of God in quietness,
in the stillness of your soul.

It is usually at dawn, when I write, dream, watch the
sunrise and am alone with myself, that I feel the
deepest and most tranquil moments of happiness.
Happiness in peace and also in action: the two must
be practiced, learned and savored as part of the art of
living.

Happiness dispels unhappiness as light dispels
    obscurity.
Therefore, switch on the happiest currents you can
    find in yourself.

Joy is my security. It creates an impenetrable shield
around me against any negative intruders.

Joy is the infallible proof of the presence of God.

Teilhard de Chardin

Decide to live joyfully,
exultantly, gratefully, openly,
and then miracles will begin to happen.

End

First you have to believe in happiness and then you will find it. It is first and foremost a question of faith.

One must try to become what the Hindus call a Trikaldarshi and a Trilokinath: one who lives happily in the past, in the present and in the future; one who lives on the ground, in the mind and in the heavens.

To give happiness is to deserve happiness.

If you have a strong dream, even it it seems an impossible one, something will happen — signs, occasions, coincidences — and help will come your way which will make your dream possible.

A world of giving and singing
and not a world of wanting and lamenting,
that should be our aim.

To seek and to find
To travel and to arrive
are both forms of happiness.

A reader wrote to me:

"I have applied your philosophy for many years in
the worst circumstances for a woman: I was happily
married to a man I loved very much. We have four
children and live in a nice house in a suburban community in the beautiful Hudson Valley. My husband's
business is in New York City. He became ever more
prosperous and one day he began to be unfaithful to
me. It was an excruciating experience, but I decided
to overcome it: I resolved that under no circumstance
would I let him take my happiness away from me. I
didn't change my attitude towards him, kept the family together, sought greater happiness from my children, my home, and my friends. Many years have
passed and very honestly I can say that I never regret-
ted my decision. He was never able to take my happiness away from me."

Happy is the person who in a dark sky rejoices at seeing a speck of light.

Norman Cousins divides the world not into East and West, North and South, black and white, but into optimists and pessimists, namely those who believe in life and those who do not. Someday, indeed, this will be the main division of humans, and someday it will disappear too, leaving only a humanity that rejoices in the miracle of life.

A few simple rules that I have found
for seeking happiness:
— good nutrition
— good thinking
— love for life
— meditation and prayer

Once during the war, a very intelligent man, a hat manufacturer from Belgium, visited our family. He heard my father complain about the hardness of the times. He went to the bathroom and brought back a fragrant bar of prewar toilet soap which my mother had extracted from her treasure chest in his honor. He passed it around and asked everyone to take a deep breath of its delightful fragrance. Then he said:

"Once this war is over never will any one of us feel again the happiness we enjoy at this moment in touching and smelling this soft, heavenly, rare bar of soap. At every time of one's life, in every circumstance, there is a certain form of happiness. The art of living consists in seeking out these special moments."

The countries of this world should not be judged by their power, their arms, and their wealth, but by the happiness of their people. What would be the point of developing the world to the standard of living existing today in the U.S. and Europe, if the people having finally reached that stage, would not be happier than are the Americans and Europeans of today?

One is great only through the cause one serves. And in our time the greatest cause can only be the peace and happiness of all humanity.

One of the happiest persons I have met in my life is Swami Satchidananda. His aim is the same as that of U Thant: to help people and humanity achieve happiness by living perfect physical, mental, moral, and spiritual lives. His name reflects his life's objective:

Sat-Chid-Ananda: Life, Knowledge, Happiness
U Thant means: the Pure

Blessed be the countries and parents who give names of virtues, Gods, and saints to their children.

We happily absorb the rays, beauty, and energy of the
    sun.
But shouldn't we radiate also something back?
Shouldn't we become a planet
radiant with peace, love, and happiness?

The world has all the bells it needs. What are missing are the hands and hearts who will make them ring
for the glory of God and of our beautiful planet.

The world is filled with people who want to dream,
to love, and to be happy. Yet happiness, love, and
dreams are nowhere to be found on the agendas of
governments and of world affairs. There must be
something wrong with this planet's politics.

Humanity must never cease to invest in new dreams
and ideals.

The whole world stops and listens when someone
comes along with the right new vision at the proper
time.

To be lasting, an artist or writer must be a prophet of good, hope, and happiness. He must deal with the essentials of life and give inspirational, uplifting, reassuring answers.

I will never know all the answers to the mysteries of life. No one ever will. But I can use my enthusiasm and talent to write and speak about the miracle of life so as to impart some happiness to my fellow humans.

To live happily, that is the success of life.

Under no circumstances need we wait for a better world to be happy and to do our duty towards the planet and humanity.

My greatest desire has always been to teach people and nations the art of happiness.

HOPE

I am sometimes called an "astonishing optimist".
What is so astonishing about being an optimist?
Is not life itself an incarnation of optimism?

A runner who wants to win a race
does not pessimistically think about defeat.
If he did he would not win.
The same is true of life.

Hope creates the image of the desired result and thus
opens the corridors of the mind to the means of its
achievement.

"Just as despair sets the stage for its own omens, so reasoned hope provides the essential nutriments for a flowering of the spirit that enhances life."

Norman Cousins

When I was a young man, I thought that at the entrance of the United Nations one should inscribe these words of Dante at the gates of hell: "You who enter here leave all hope."

Now at the end of my journey, I think that one should inscribe instead the following words: "You who enter here never lose hope."

Have a dream and believe deeply in it.
Strong dreams always come true.

LOVE

There is only one great law in life:
the law of love for everything we do.

If I love life, then life will be beautiful.
If I love my family, I will have a happy family.
If I love my work, I will be successful.
If I love my house, I will have a beautiful home.
If I love to study, to write, to read,
to paint, to sculpt,
to garden, to sing, to walk,
my life will be happier through these activities.
If I love God, I will find an ultimate happiness.

Love is simply the joy of being fully what we are meant to be.

To love is to give reality and worth to someone or something.

At the beginning of human evolution, knowledge and love were synonymous. Then they became separate. Nothing could be more important than to reunite them again.

A genius without heart is non-sense.

Mozart

Whenever I have found beauty in life,
there was a great act of love at the origin.

As the eye encompasses in one view
millions of bits of perception,
so can our heart encompass in one stroke of love
the wondrous complexity of life and Creation.

You may love the detail. But as with a work of art, do not forget to contemplate the totality, the universal.

One can see too much, read too much,
learn too much, talk too much,
but one can never love too much.

Life is giving and receiving,
reflecting and absorbing.

Never get weary of giving and you will never cease to
receive.

Where there is love, there is no obligation.

Love is the only treasure that the rich cannot steal
from the poor.

Peace, love, and brotherhood cannot be "organized".
These qualities must grow in the heart of each human
being. You are their only creator.

To love peace is not enough.
We are asked to let love transform us from within,
into the powerful peacemakers that we really can be.

Humans are mirrors: they reflect my fist or my smile.

Human relations on this planet are too cold. We must
warm them up. The temperature of international relations, in particular, must be raised to a germinating
level. The human ice age and its cold wars have lasted
much too long. This must be the responsibility of
each of us. Any personal warmth we can contribute
to human relations will raise the general temperature
of the world society. How can we expect nations to
be loving and compassionate if we are not loving and
compassionate ourselves?

Arnold Toynbee once was asked what he would recommend as the single most important means for achieving a better world. He answered: "If only people could be kinder to each other."

The love of country has succeeded in binding people at the national level. The great new historical challenge is to develop love among all Earth inhabitants and for the Earth itself.

The world must now acquire a heart and a soul.

I dream of a world in which no bird would fly away and no animal flee at the approach of a human.

We speak 5,000 different languages but our hearts beat the same.

In the end it is those who have dreamed and loved the strongest who will survive the longest in the memory of humanity.

We need more than a world vision (*Weltanschauung*). We need a world love (*Weltliebe*).

Perhaps only through love and transcendence can we get close to perceiving the ultimate mystery. *Sursum corda*, Lift up your hearts in order to see and unite yourselves to the universe.

After a life of thinking and searching, I found love as the ultimate answer:
love for the whole Creation and its mysterious source;
love for our beautiful planet and for all its living beings;
love for my own miraculous life and for all the loves I feel in me.
This is what I felt when I was a child.
Now the circle is complete.

We become what we love.

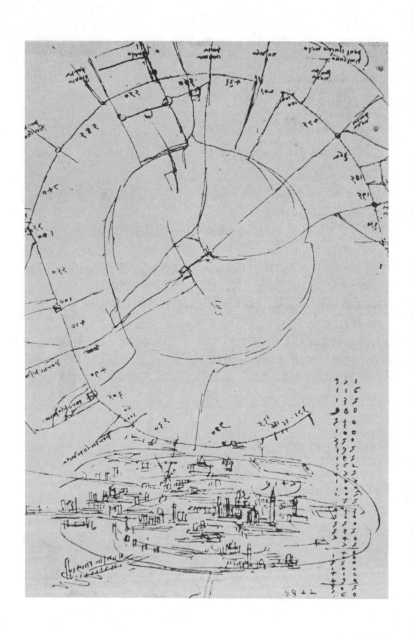

CHAPTER THREE

ON WRITING
AND SPEAKING

To write and to speak are primarily an expansion and observation of life, a two-way process of learning, teaching, communicating, and contributing to human progress and happiness. Therefore, do not become a writer or speaker for writing's or speaking's sake, but as a means of fulfilling yourself and bringing happiness, joy, and goodness to others.

Writing conserves. It is a form of eternity, of capturing time, preserving individual and collective lives, knowledge, and history. How precious writing can be...

Hidden wisdom is no good. Every wise person must publish his wisdom through speaking, writing, action, storytelling at every stage of his life.

Don't be only consumers. Don't read newspapers and books or watch television all the time. Produce something. Write down your thoughts, feelings, and memories. It will validate your life and make you feel great.

The most fundamental form of writing is the journal as a means of observing the functioning of your being, your heart, your mind, and your senses in relation to the surrounding world, the living and the dead, the past, the present, and the future. The journal is the key, the great secret, to experiencing the joy of writing and living.

Do not lose hope when you begin to write. When I read the beginning of my journal many years ago, I felt like throwing it into the waste basket. It was so terribly bad! But then I thought that it was my life that was concerned. And with time, experience, and patience, I also learned beauty. Corrected and improved, the first days of my journal are today one of my greatest treasures.

One can write almost anywhere: at a meeting, on a train, in a plane, in public or in your home. You could not sculpt or paint or practice any other art with such facility. I have told my children: "Write whenever you can, as much as you can, wherever you are. Record your life, your experiences, your thoughts, your observations, and your dreams. You will learn much about the world, the universe, and yourself."

To write is to live twice.
To keep a journal is to live many, many times.

Nulla dies sine linea.
No day without a line.

Verba volant, scripta manent.
Words fly away. Writings remain.

Walking from my home to the railroad station, I had a marvelous thought. I did not write it down and so I have lost it. Now I always carry with me a piece of paper to note the flashes of truth that come to mind.

Write in order to know yourself;
write to help your human brothers and sisters;
write to give happiness to others;
but never write purely for fame or glory.

I write only about what I love. What happens to the fruit is not a matter of concern to the tree.

To write is to be at maximum truth with oneself, the purest form of living.

When others read me, they must feel as if I had written for them; for even when I am writing for myself, I am writing for all other human beings. To explore one's soul as a writer is to meet with the soul of all humanity.

The most rewarding books are those which render other people happy.

We can be greater writers and speakers than any others in history, because we know so much more and live in a greater world.

Never underestimate letter writing: another human being will read you, might be moved by you and may spread your message if it is an honest and basic truth.

There is no born writer. Shakespeare was once a child who could not write. Do not be afraid of your "bad style". Continue, and with time you will improve through craftsmanship, like any artist or artisan. Do not see the bad product of today but the beauty of tomorrow.

Reread what you write, correct it, chisel it, polish it time and again until *you* are satisfied that nothing should be changed, that it is the most perfect work you can produce.

A painter will never paint all he wants to paint.
A writer will never write all he wants to write.
A composer will never compose all he wants to
   compose.
Once a skill is mastered and has become second
   nature,
there is no end to what you can and want to do with
   it.

Write, write, write.
Paint, paint, paint.
Michelangelo refused the Pope's invitations to
   dinner with this comment:
"Do you want me to paint or to have dinner with
   you?"
He slept in the Sistine Chapel with his paints and
   lived to the age of 90.

Poetry is a way of seeing and writing to better understand and feel the greatness, the breadth, the depth,
and the intensity of the miracle of life.

One of the great joys on Earth is the birth of a book.

A good writer must give firm hope and crystal-clear happiness. A reader wants to be reassured about life: aggrandized, not diminished and confused. Why should he receive your unhappiness and negativity? He has enough of them himself. You might interest him, but he will put your book aside and never return to it. He will re-read only positive, hopeful, helpful books.

Writings are preserved life. Books are preserved people. Books of quotations and sayings by great authors represent an incredible amount of life experience.

If only all the heads of state and of world agencies jotted down a few of their philosophical thoughts, wisdom, perceptions, ideas, and conclusions, as Dag Hammarskjöld did in his *Markings*, what a richer world it would be! They live in a vaster world, with vaster duties and a vaster audience than any Socrates, Confucius, Marcus Aurelius or Lincoln. The world needs a true global literature written by authors who have deeply lived and received the new universal currents which have seized this planet and the human race.

We do not want any young person to say in the future: "Why didn't you write it all down? You should have known that I would be coming along."

I always take solace from the fact that St. Augustine started to write the *City of God* at the age of 59!

Churchbells, gongs, tom-toms, shofars, muezzins, mountain horns, and sung music are all vibrations which help us to feel at one with the universe. So are great speeches, books, and works of art.

Speaking and language are powerful cosmic vibrations, which we must treat with reverence and respect, using their positive, while avoiding their negative aspects. We should never employ violent language.

The Indians know about the power of language: Sanskrit rightly means "divine language". *Dewanagara*, the script in which it is embodied, means "the city of God" (*Dewa*: God; *nagara*: city).

We must learn to speak and listen not only to others, but to ourselves.

When speaking and writing, I always try to validate and elevate those who hear or read me.

When you listen to me, when you read me, you do not merely give me your attention and your time; you give me part of your most precious possession: your life. My communication with you must therefore be as precious as your life.

There is something I admire about IBM: after each lecture or seminar I give to their high officials from around the world, I receive an evaluation of my effectiveness and performance by each participant. This permits me to improve myself, to change course if I went wrong, to adapt myself to the needs of a special profession, and to do better next time. Alas, how many times in my life have I been asked for my opinion about goods, services, teachers, publishers, supervisors, books, films, etc.? I feel that all my life I have been a captive consumer.

The miracle of spontaneous creation: often, after a speech, I return to my office and I say to my secretary: "I learned so much today listening to myself!" There are indeed moments when I feel that another being is speaking through me, that a mysterious knowledge or enlightenment manifests itself in me spontaneously, without any intervention of my will or thought. I stand there, speak, and listen like a captive student to what wells up in me and comes to my lips. Like water, like matter, we partake in a common intelligence and heart. To young inspired speakers who produce unexpected thoughts and sentences I say: "Always carry a tape recorder with you, record your speeches and guard the tapes carefully. You will discover something worth more to you than gold."

O, God, help us to reach far beyond what we are saying. Isn't it possible to unlock the ultimate mystery,
to become You?

I feel like writing an Appeal to Humanity, to all human brothers and sisters, asking them to take things
into their own hands, for the people are closer to the
truth than their governments.

I will repeat and repeat what I have to say again and
again until nations will listen and change.

CHAPTER FOUR

ON GROWTH AND EVOLUTION

It is no accident that we are alive.
I cannot accept that the occurrence of our planet in
  the universe
and the appearance of life on it
are a pure accident and have no particular,
  extraordinary sense.

There are scientists who believe that everything can be explained by evolution. Yet evolution as we understand it represents only a few hundred million years on our small planet in a minor solar system in one corner of the universe. Creation is infinitely vaster and more mysterious than we can conceive.

This does not mean that we are not a marvelous planet, a tremendous achievement, a true jewel in the universe. Everything in Creation is a manifestation of a sublime cosmic force, but we must not have the arrogance to believe that life on our planet can fit into a finite theory of evolution. There is infinitely more in the heavens and on Earth than in any human theory.

Suppose the universe is producing innumerable stars — like a fish innumerable eggs — to heat innumerable planets for billions of years until one of them at long last produces a miracle: life is born, matter and energy become life, evolution into ever more complex and marvelous forms begins! What a responsibility that would mean for our present nuclear powers! What a change of politics, attitudes and values it would require!

Our planet is so small and part of such a tiny solar system among trillions of solar systems of a small galaxy among trillions of galaxies that our efforts to understand Creation resemble those of a flea trying to comprehend planet Earth.

The spinning of our planet around the sun seems immense to us. And yet, in the vast universe, it is so small that we cannot even be distinguished from our sun. At a distance of a few light years, our planet becomes invisible, a mere grain of dust or nothingness. And yet, we exist . . .

There is not a single encyclopedia on this Earth which presents our total knowledge within the two most obvious and logical frameworks that press themselves upon us so glaringly, namely: the total universe, i.e., from the infinitely large to the infinitely small; and total time, i.e., from the infinite past to the infinite future.

You cannot understand the greatness of the universe if you do not constantly lift yourself up to it. This is why we look for God in the heavens.

We are minuscule prisoners of the universe and of time. We will never understand the infinitely large and infinitely small. And yet, within these colossal limitations we can live searching, joyous, confident, divine lives. As Blake wrote: "If the sun and moon should doubt, they'd immediately go out."

Life! It begins when a divine, ecstatic moment of love releases a tiny, wiggling sperm towards an egg. These absorb matter and energy and become a colossal mass of conscious life in the universe!

We are so lucky in the universe: a few thousand miles further from our sun and we would freeze; a few thousand miles closer and we would burn. We must therefore remember at all times that our planet is a true miracle and that God must have a very special design for us on it. The definition of that design is one of the paramount duties of our age. What does God, what does the cosmos or universe expect from us and from our further evolution?

Human evolution began when the first human being looked up at the stars; we were a planet of passive, non-questioning, nontransforming beings until one day, suddenly, in one of the humans a spark, similar to the spark which gave birth to life, arose: the first question. "What is that? Why are we naked?" In the beginning was the word. A whole new page of evolution started from that day: the transformation of a planet through one of its species, the self-consciousness of the universe in that species, a rare phenomenon in the cosmos, the future course of which lies entirely in our hands. What an awe-inspiring challenge! What a responsibility for our species! All preceding values are superseded by this new task.

Each of us can be and should be a precious contribution to human evolution in the cosmos. Seen in the four infinites, human life becomes a tremendous privilege. We could as well have never been born and never received the gift of life in the vast universe and eternity. We must therefore act so as to merit our lives and contribute to a higher level of evolution. This ancient religious truth is beginning to reappear in the theory of "genetic codification".

If, as is the case, everything on this planet is a coagulation or form of cosmic forces, then we might as well have an immense respect for everything we see, including ourselves. A grain of dust, a flower, a drop of water are not just anything. They are miracles demanding our astonishment. And most astonishing of all are humans, who through searching, questioning, and reasoning are ever expanding the consciousness of the universe.

I cannot repeat it enough.
The great secret is this:
consider yourself a part of the universe
and a part of the eternal stream of time.
Consider your life to be a true miracle;
and put to God all the questions you may have.

To be fully human, we must tap into the primal energy of the universe. Plato held that the soul of the universe, incarnated in a human being, lost much of its qualities and became imperfect. The effort of human beings should be to strive back to the perfection of the soul and to feel part of the mysterious flows and throbbing life of the universe.

It takes a great act of courage to try to make sense of life and Creation; it requires faith, love, passion, enthusiasm, poetry, and music as well as mathematics and scientific ability. There is as much in Shakespeare and Beethoven as in Darwin and Einstein. I sometimes wonder if humanity would not be better off in foregoing its investigations and conquests of the infinitely large and small. We could as well be content with seeing reality as it appears in all its beauty and simplicity. For will we ever be able to control the forces we unlock? That is the great question of our future.

Learn with all your heart and soul from the treasures of your own experience. There is no greater master than your own life and journey in time and space.

Each human being is a prism in which the whole universe is reflected.

We are only a drop of water in the ocean of humanity, but without drops of water there would be no ocean.

I have tried all my life to increase humanity's receptivity to the fact that we are a true miracle in the universe, a unique species living on an astonishing planet.

Fullest possible consciousness, that is the purpose of life. Fullest possible consciousness for all, that is the purpose of evolution. This is the last great jump to be made by our otherwise materially and intellectually fairly well-developed human race.

So many people seek cosmic union or to see the bright, divine light, a transcendence, something superior, "higher". But suppose we saw this planet from "below" in the universe and considered it as a tremendous success of the bright light or divine energy having become matter and life, especially human life? Then it would be this life, *our* life, which would appear as ultimate bliss, a reflection of transcendence, something "higher".

Humanity as an entity is only beginning to take shape and to evolve: it begins to have common perceptions of reality, common feelings and common concerns; it begins to act and react as one body to common dangers and events, to evolve towards higher forms of coordinated action and fulfillment in total cosmic reality. In this evolution all former primitive groups and beliefs will have to adapt or perish.

Power is a desire of the primitive, unevolved human being.

Humanity has many rights and aspirations,
   but not the right to commit suicide.
It took us too long and too much work to get where
   we are.

Why should a government born yesterday, a nation born only a few hundred years ago, an ideology unknown last century, a religion at best a few thousand years old be more valuable than human life, especially the life born from me? This planet is 4.5 billion years old and human life has existed for 3 million years. They are my primary concern. No person, no law, no government, no institution, no enterprise, no religion, no ideology should ever be allowed to endanger and to destroy this planet and human life. My first and foremost human right is the right not to kill and not to be killed by anyone. A new political, planetary order must be built on that right.

Nothing contrary to evolution can last for long. Revolutions and evolution constantly change the human fabric until the basic harmonies and optimum fulfillment are achieved. At present we are witnessing a basic evolution against the unnatural cutting up of the world into nations.

Nature all around us is so beautiful. It is real magic. But what is behind it is probably even more beautiful. It is that transcendent beauty and meaning which we must seek at this stage of our evolution. And for that purpose we must settle our earthly problems and differences as quickly as possible. We are losing much precious time.

To the natural, ecological, political, and economic interdependence of our planet, one must add a newcomer: the interdependence of feelings. People are no longer ignorant and insensitive to any great cataclysm or misery occurring elsewhere in the world. Ours has become a feeling, a sensitive planet, a heavenly body with a heart of its own.

This planet needed a bloodstream, a nervous system, a brain, a heart, and a soul. It developed the human species for that purpose, and it took only a short evolutionary period of three million years for humans to reach the stage when today we can perform these tasks.

We must never forget that the world is engaged in one gigantic effort to find its fulfillment, and we must each bring our share to it.

A genius is never proud and erect, but always on his knees, in full admiration of the greatness of the universe.

Science is related to religion because it is an attempt to understand our cosmic home. The first scientists were astronomerpriests. The separation of science and spirituality is one of the most monumental aberrations in human history.

When I look at the little head of a parrot, of a dog, or a cat, I thank God for having given me a human brain which can encompass so much of the universe. But then I think that the human head is still so tiny that it can understand only an infinitesimal part of infinite Creation. What is our ultimate reality, out there, beyond the limits of our comprehension?

To count the grains of all the sands of our planet would yield an infinite number.

To count the drops of water of all the seas and oceans would give an infinite number.

To count all the molecules of the Earth's atmosphere would produce an infinite number.

To count all the atoms of the sands, water, air, rocks, plants, and beings of our planet would yield an infinite number.

And yet, in the infinite universe, our planet is but a tiny drop of matter.

On this droplet of matter, humans feel, love, dream, think, and act like semi-Gods.

And among those four billion fellow humans I am unique, unrepeatable, a world or cosmos of my own linked with all there is in the heavens and on Earth.

And the greatest marvel of all is that I can comprehend and conceive what I have just written.

The first thing we see when we meet a human person is that he is alive. Those who are sick and dying are out of sight: they are in their homes or in hospitals, and those who are dead have been taken away permanently. They are gone forever. Hence the supreme value for humans is life itself, not youth, not beauty, not intelligence, not prosperity. A poor, old, ugly, living person has an immense advantage over a dead child or a dead beautiful woman or a dead rich man. Therefore, the great truth for us is not, "I think, therefore I am", but "I live, therefore I am".

To be alive or not to be alive, that is the question.

In the vast universe, we humans are true kings, almost Gods. We know so much, feel so much, dream so much, query so much, discover so much. We will not rest lest we see, know, feel, and understand all we can in the heavens and on Earth. Being of divine or cosmic origin, we want to return to the outer expanses of the universe from whence we have come. We are a transcending species capable of lifting itself beyond its capacities and senses by a truly miraculous urge. We are stupendous little nebulae of life on a little rocky and watery planet, trying to reach out for the stars and the outer limits of heaven. What a prodigious species we are! What a teeming laboratory our planet is in the vast universe! And how could it be otherwise, since we are energy, matter, and soul from the universe which has passed through many starforms before our present planetary embodiment. Hence the instinct of our divine and cosmic nature, hence our longing for the heavens.

Given the constant beating we are giving to our body, nerves, heart, mind, and spirit, it appears that a human being is the incarnation of a tremendous, renewable force of will for life. The cosmos must therefore be trying to achieve something special through the human race. Our reponsibilities may reach far beyond anything we have ever dreamt heretofore and which has been understood only by the great seers and prophets.

Use the cosmic energy in you. Attract it like a magnet for the benefit of all. Cosmic energy is seeking to build. If it feels that you are a builder, it will come to you. If you ignore it, it will flee you. We have not yet learned to use the cosmic, divine forces in and around us.

If we are matter of the Earth, if we are cosmic matter become conscious of itself, then it is our duty to manage this planet so as to maximize its consciousness in the universe. That might be the purpose of all evolution. A new science and art of consciousness must be developed: the transformation of the Earth into a highly conscious cell of the universe.

There is enough spiritual power locked in this Earth to lift the human race into the universe. Perhaps the human race is Earth become spirit.

The Earth is more likely to stop rotating than humanity to stop progressing.

At our stage of evolution, there will be growing numbers of enlightened, universal beings. Some day peaceful, serene saints will be the majority of this Earth's inhabitants.

Is there a supreme consciousness?
Why has the universe or God or evolution created
　　human life?
What can be my satisfactory answers to these
　　momentous questions?
I do not know, but of one thing I am sure:
My reason, my science, my art, my love, my religion,
　　my poetry, and my philosophy
　　are all expressions of respect
　　for the magnificence of Creation.

What is God, if not the ultimate force and logic that
holds the universe together? How can we live without
believing that such a logic exists? The notion of God
is for me indispensable. He would not have been invented so many times in history if there had not been
a real necessity for Him.

The whole purpose of human evolution is to draw us nearer to God in resembling Him, each according to his own nature. Thus will we reach our perfection and fulfill our cosmic function.

The human person has been created to feel and serve the greatness of the universe and of infinity, i.e., to fulfill the will of God.

We live in the universe. Hence we are universal beings. We must pursue our evolutionary elevation into fully transcended cosmic beings. We may be a life form at the spearhead of evolution in the universe. It is our duty towards the universe from which we have received everything to fulfill our cosmic destiny. Alas, we have not even tried to define that destiny!

In the end, everything adapts and flows into the great Heraclitean stream of history and evolution. No nation, no group, no power, no wealth, no ideology remains eternal. And yet they all believe they are eternal. Only the Earth and humanity remain.

We are a journey towards universal symphony and harmony.

Ask yourself the question:
"Would I like to return to Earth and live again?"
The answer will throw important light on your life.

It makes us fearful to think of death.
But if one thinks of one's life as a service,
as a contribution to human ascent and evolution,
as part of the flow of the mysterious universe,
then death is only a transformation,
a change of being.

To seek is not enough. We must also find.

To believe in our further evolution is the key to humanity's success. We absolutely must believe.

CHAPTER FIVE

THE WORK FOR PEACE

From the notion of sickness we have at long last passed to the concept of health as the normal condition of a human person. Similarly, we must now pass from the notion of conflict to that of peace as the normal condition of humanity.

What is my first recommendation for peace? That it be practiced and taught in each family, where the leaders, educators and adults of tomorrow will all come from.

Peace cannot be taken in isolation: hunger, oppression, injustice, unemployment, lack of meaning are all causes of conflict. To work on these causes is therefore to work for peace.

Loving peace is not enough. We also need a peace-making vision, science, strategy, and action.

O, leaders of nations, you have no right to destroy this planet, because you have not created it.

O, leaders of nations, you have no right to destroy humanity, because you have not created it.

O, leaders of nations, you have no right to get me killed, because you have not created me.

No one has given the right to the big nuclear powers to decide our fate. Who are they anyway to endanger innocent populations for the sake of their interests and power?

Everybody wants a better world. But who is ready to accept that to be human is more important than to be American, Russian, Arab, Jewish, Catholic, or Protestant? And yet, it will be a better world only when people will have made this fundamental conversion to the truth.

Now that the world has a United Nations with rules of conflict resolution, no war is a just war.

The arms race is like economics, you hear the most sophisticated, intelligent, endlessly complicated statements and theories, but basically it is *all wrong*. It would be infinitely better for these fine minds to begin working on planetary management.

I dream of a university in which each chair would bear the name of a famous peacemaker.

The time absolutely must come when the world spends on peace what it now spends on war.

Even if unused, armaments kill: they kill little children who could have been saved if resources spent on arms had been available for their nourishment and care.

Outcries against injustice resemble pain in the human body: they point at a malfunctioning of the system.

Peace is not only the absence of war, it is a human virtue and morality that can be radiated by all living humans. Peace as non-war is a pretty poor concept, and yet what a great first step it would be!

The peace of the world is the sum-total of the peace of all people.

First you have to disarm your minds.

No nation or human group ever remains at the top for long. Power provokes jealousy, competition and alliances from without: remember the story of Gulliver and the Lilliputians. Power also dissolves from within; it engenders its own parasites which feed on its substance. The problem henceforth is how to achieve and maintain a peaceful, happy, world-wide human society. That is the great historic current which is shaking the present world political structure. The games of nations will soon be over.

An Indian chief said to me: "Humanity is one nation with many tribes." Indeed, we should call only humanity a nation, the human nation, and call all others tribes. The United Nations must become the United Nation.

"The sword will always be conquered by the spirit."

Napoleon

I prefer any honest pure atheist to a religious bigot ready to go to war for his religion.

For God and humanity,
Not for God and my country.

What is more important, life or your nationality?
If you take away my passport, I will still have my
precious life.
If you take away my life, you can throw my passport
in the trashcan.
Hence, my life is more important than my
nationality.

A hundred years ago, Madame de Staël wrote that
three main reasons led men to war: the love for father-
land and liberty, the love of glory, and religious fanaticism. Today, the second reason has disappeared: no
one can find glory any more in war. Religious fanaticism has diminished, but not disappeared. Strongest
today are still love for country and liberty. One could
add two new causes: love for justice and ideological
fanaticism.

If anyone decided to create an institute for the comparative study of Communism and Capitalism, both would scream: "But this is impossible. We hold the perfect truth. If everybody follows us, we will achieve peace and happiness on Earth." Of course. All the religions said the same and then killed each other for centuries in the name of a total, infallible truth. At this period of human evolution, we must reject and outgrow such naiveté. The management of this Earth and of billions of people is infinitely more complex than the theorists of Liberalism and Socialism could have dreamt 100 years ago. They would be the first to scrap their theories if they returned to life.

Thank God that we have Socialism to remind us of the human dream of equality and that we have the free enterprise system to remind us of the human dream of liberty. Why can't they join hands together?

A planet which spends 2,500 times more on armaments than on peacekeeping and as little on health and education is not a well-run planet. Governments deserve an F in planetary management.

The strangest of all entities ever invented is the
  Nation.
And they happen to be strongest today at the time
  when they are
most unnatural and least needed.

Don't be black or white before being human.
Don't be a Catholic or a Jew before being human.
Don't be American or Russian before being
  human.
Don't be European or Asian before being human.
Don't be Communist or Capitalist before being
  human.
For the first time in history, to be human comes
  first.
Only thus can the people save this planet.

Ours is *not* the age of reason. How could it be, with
its atomic bombs, its conflicts, its hatred, its pover-
ty, its dying children, its hunger, its innumerable un-
needed and unemployed? It should rather be called the
century of global horror.

I once asked a young man: "Are you a human being?" He answered: "Of course I am." "No, you are a national being, because if tomorrow you are ordered by your nation to kill another human being, you will do so. Hence you are first and foremost a national being and not a human being."

It is shattering that two antiquated ideologies based on wealth and power should occupy the forefront of the world scene at such a delicate, momentous juncture of our cosmic evolution.

Ambassador Belaunde from Peru once said: "When there is a problem between two small nations, the problem disappears. When there is a problem between a big country and a small country, the little country disappears. When there is a problem between two big countries, the United Nations disappears."

When the Bangla-Desh upheaval broke out, the Ambassador of Pakistan exclaimed in response to a speech by India: "What you call right to self-determination, we call treason." How many times do we see people called patriots by one side and traitors by the other! This can end only after humanity has organized itself into one family under one government, one world morality, and one world law and ethics. The world's 150-plus national minorities must be molded into one Earth community.

This planet belongs to no one.

Human government still remains at the surface of things. It has hardly any depth. If it had, there would be no war and armaments on this planet.

The world and humanity badly need a system of world law and justice. For example, it might nationally be "legal" for someone to join an army and to kill other human beings. But from humanity's point of view, such killing constitutes murder. What is true and legal within a nation can be no less true within the entire human family.

This ancient text still applies to state behaviour and to terrorism:

"When Alexander the Great asked a captured pirate what he meant by infesting the sea, the pirate boldly replied: "And what do you mean by warring on the whole world? I do my fighting on a tiny ship, and they call me a pirate; you do yours with a large fleet, and they call you a Commander".

St. Augustine, The City of God, Book 4.

War, violence and terrorism will continue as long as people will tolerate them. The sucessful movement of the 19th Century to abolish slavery must be followed by peoples' movements

> to abolish war
> to abolish violence
> to abolish terrorism.

People should take their power back from governments who kill or practice violence.

Each individual on Earth should interrupt his activities at least for a few seconds every day to think about peace. This alone would change the course of the world.

What we are witnessing these days is the eradication of war from the values of humanity. This will have momentous effects.

The more interdependent the world becomes, the less there will be risk of war. International business networks and associations are therefore very vital peacemakers.

Wherever there is love, there is peace.

Burmese proverb often quoted by U Thant

More than anything else, persons of wealth and power want to sever us from two things, nature and the soul, for both speak of peace and simple living.

Peace is not only outward but also within us, in the innermost depth of our soul. Individual peace therefore is the product of individual spirituality, and world peace is the product of world spirituality.

All life is flow. I must therefore flow peacefully and not be hard like rock.

Peacemakers perform the most advanced cosmic function. They are the ultimate instruments and the fulfillment of the divine nature. This is why in all religions they are considered the highest, the most beloved, among the saints and the immortals.

All humans meet at the deeper levels of prayer and in the common experience of God. Hence, only a world spirituality can save humanity from its quandaries.

So many unimportant things are being presented to us as important that we are finally completely taken away from the essence of life which is to be in communion with God, with nature, with each other, with the heavens and with eternity. Our divinity is being crushed by noise, untruths and unnecessary ways of life. We must revolt and protect our importance and divinity.

There will be no true justice, peace, and happiness on this planet as long as we do not submit to the laws of God. The religions do not matter: they are only ways, indeed beautifully diverse ways as are all ways of nature, to the same fundamental truth and unity. We must again place this planet under the protective wing of God.

We must seek full employment for the masses of saints and good spirits who linger around this planet. They are eager to help us defeat the forces of evil, but if *uncalled* they are powerless.

Society can never consider individual human life as precious enough.

In the final battle for this planet between the forces of evil and good, no one can be neutral.

CHAPTER SIX

THE GLOBAL AGE

For most of human history, people thought that the Earth was the center of the universe. Then we learned that the sun was not turning around the Earth but that the Earth was circling around the sun. So we thought that the sun was the center of the universe. Then we learned that the sun is only a small star turning around one of the axes of a galaxy. Then we learned that this galaxy is circling around the pole of a cluster of galaxies which in turn is rotating around the pole of a spheric expanding universe! How small and diminished we have become! Scientists further tell us that time, distance, speed, mass, and energy are all relative. But, if this is so, then perhaps we are not so small after all! We might even be the only living planet in a universe of fire, gases, atomic explosions, and interstellar voids! Our conditions might be unique: the right distance from a sun not to burn and not to freeze, the right mass to retain our water and atmosphere, the right rotation and orbit, the right atomic density and chemical composition. So we might after all be the center of the universe, a unique, miraculous planet on which the Creator has a special eye. What responsibility this would mean for us! What change of thinking, concern, policies and behavior it would require from our political leaders! What immense human pride, gratitude and truly religious feeling it would imply from us!

Leibniz rightly predicted that for hundreds of years we would be so busy with science and technology that we would lose all sense of the universal. But the time would return when humanity, bewildered by the complexity of our knowledge, would yearn again for a universal synthesis and vision. That time has come.

An important recent view has been to see the entire history of our planet reduced to the span of one day: the birth of the human race occurs only 5 minutes before midnight and the industrial civilization only at the first stroke of the clock at 12. Another view is to see that we have still two long days before us and that this first stroke of midnight is in reality the first strike of the global age.

We wrongly say: we live on this planet.
We must say: we are part of this planet,
in flesh, in liquids, in air,
in mind, in heart, in life, and in death.
We are part of this universe for all eternity.

Once when I delivered a speech, a young man put in front of me a cosmic clock which showed the speed at which the Earth was rotating around itself, around the sun, and around our galactic center. When I finished speaking, I could see the millions of miles covered in the meantime by our little globe in the vast universe!

Our world family of several billion individuals on one little planet in the fathomless universe and eternal stream of time, that is the central challenge of tomorrow's Earth's government.

I would advise every searching human being to place his search and to search his place within four general frameworks:

> the total universe
> total time
> the total Earth
> the total human family.

We have made great progress of late toward the concept and concern of the whole Earth or globe or planet. We must make similar progress towards the concept and concern of Whole Humanity or global human race or planetary dwellers.

Perhaps in the evolution of the universe there comes a time when a species has unriddled most secrets of its environment and begins to become the master and manager of a planet. We seem to have reached that stage in our evolution.

Beyond world federalism and world government we need first and foremost a world democracy, a government of this planet for the people and by the people. But the problem is so colossal and unprecedented that few political thinkers even dare to consider it. They feel more at ease discussing the number and strength of missiles needed to protect specific national corrals. Since government and institutions are so slow and reluctant to do it, we must build the world community through individual commitment and action.

The greatest wisdom of all required at this point of our evolution is world wisdom, namely the ability to distinguish between what is good and bad for humanity. We need philosophers at the helm of nations and institutions.

Nations beware:
  people will form themselves into one humanity
  whatever you may think or do.
  No one can stop evolution.

This is a good planet for humans: it provides endless room for human curiosity and for participation in the process of continued Creation and evolution. The greatest task confronting us is to determine what the right future should be.

This planet must be managed so that each individual human life can be a great work of art.

Global education and global communications are the two breasts which will nurture our entry into the global phase of evolution. Cosmic education and communications are waiting around the corner to nurture the next one.

We must find the rules and laws of the universe as they apply to our planet.

Only the unity of all can bring the well-being of all.

Again today I will travel by plane from Europe to North America. But it will be the same sun, the same source of life, light and energy which will shine for me. If we could only have a solar view of our planet.

No country is the last corner on Earth, because the Earth is round and has no corners.

If only we could look at the beauty of our life, of this planet, and of humanity as we would look at the beauty of a mountain: seeing the total majesty, not the irregularities.

Wrong education is the principal cause of the political disorder on this planet. People with a limited vision can only produce limited solutions. We need on this planet hosts of people with a world vision. If your child was taught that Westchester County is the most important place on Earth and that out there is the rest of the world, you would protest with anger, and yet this is how most children are still educated about their own nations.

Once you have seen a picture of this planet from outer space, you will never be the same person again.

It is strange: one could not envisage for a moment a household, a city, a school, a firm, a factory, a farm, an institution, a religion, or a nation without a head, a principal, a manager, an administrator, or a government. But we accept readily that the world can be left without one! We should not be surprised, therefore, that there are so many wars, acts of violence, and global crises on this planet.

I wish the people of this planet would cease to belong to groups of "special people" who proclaim that they are superior to others and that they hold the ultimate truth given to them by nature, by God, by sacred scriptures, or by social reformers. If we found another planet in the universe with so many "ultimate truths" — economic, social, or religious — we would consider its people crazy and would ask them to put their house in order. Why don't we start doing that on our own planet?

After the Peking man, after the Neanderthal man, after the Cro-Magnon man, after the cave man, we are now witnessing the birth of the One-world person.

The really underdeveloped people on this planet are those who have no world consciousness.

We are a very developed planet scientifically and technologically, but a most underdeveloped planet politically, morally, sentimentally and spiritually. These should be our new priorities. What wonders we will achieve once we devote to them our intelligence and imagination!

If our globe could speak, it would say to us:

"You make me laugh, you humans. I have been twirling around for four and a half billion years. I have seen many upheavals in my flesh; I have seen continents disappear, seas change place, mountains surge, ice covers come and go, an atmosphere be born, vegetation arise, life develop, species evolve and disappear. You came into being only two or three million years ago. I have seen you crawl in utter ignorance for most of this time. Only a few hundred years ago did you at long last discover that I was round and older than just a few thousand years. I have been observing you, and I want to tell you this: You will go nowhere if you do not remember that I will be around for several billion years more, that my body will be shaken by many more climatic changes, that for your maximum enjoyment and survival you must treat and manage me with care, that you must increasingly put yourself in my place and lift your eyes as I do to the sun, to the universe, to infinity and eternity, of which I am only a tiny cell. After your cave age, after your crawling age, after your tribal age, after your feudal age, after your national age, you have at long last entered *my* age: the global age. But this is still insufficient, for you will have to enter the cosmic age in which you will see your proper place in the total universe and time. This is the next great stage of your prodigious journey."

Conflicts will diminish as our global, universal, spiritual, and cosmic awareness increase. By far the greatest contribution to peace an individual can make is to become a global, universal, spiritual, and cosmic being.

A synthesis between the past and the future
       "   "   east and west
       "   "   north and south
       "   "   science and religion
       "   "   the heavens and the earth

that is the major task of our generation.

At this stage of our evolution, we are in the midst of creating a whole series of world-wide communities:

a world-wide community of knowledge,
       "   "   of concern,
       "   "   of conscience,
       "   "   of care,
       "   "   of love,
       "   "   of action.

There is always some area to which we can actively contribute.

When humanity will have solved its material problems, its intellectual problems, and its moral problems, it will at last be faced with the most fundamental question of all: the spiritual quest, namely—what is our place in the universe and in time? Then will start the cosmic age of our fabulous journey. Then we will find at long last the right answers to all our problems.

The galaxies move around the central axis of the universe according to fixed laws. Our planet turns around the sun according to fixed laws. The whole universe is ruled by laws. Should we not assume therefore that we too are expected to live according to fixed cosmic laws? Do we think that we are free to act as we deem fit? This would not be freedom, but breaking the law, with our destruction as the consequence. Beautiful, satisfying music requires the search for the laws of harmony. Similarly, a beautiful, satisfying human society will require the search for the laws of harmony of the universe. This will be the role of tomorrow's universal, cosmic government.

Intellectual qualities are superior to physical qualities; moral qualities are superior to intellectual qualities; and spiritual qualities are the highest of all. This is borne out by our daily observations: a person endowed with a good physique and a fine mind is superior to one having only a good body; a person who has also good moral qualities is superior to the former; and the most admirable person of all is the one who has a good physique, a great intelligence, and a good heart, and who is spiritually in communion with God and the universe. The same is true of any social group, from the family to the entire human race. Our present human family is still very imperfect because:

— it has not yet assured good physical lives to all its four and a half billion people: 500 million of them still go hungry;

— it has not yet provided for good mental lives for all: there are still one billion illiterates on this planet;

— it has not yet become a moral world: there are still too many conflicts, injustices, inequalities, violence, hatred, lies, miseducation, misinformation, and dishonesty;

— it is not yet a spiritual world: we still relate everything to earthly concerns and seldom lift our minds, hearts, and souls to the universe and to the eternal stream of time. Our planet has yet to become the Planet of God.

The dream to understand our place in the universe breaks through all barriers. It binds the people together. Hence the need for a global philosophy and spirituality.

We must combine ancient wisdom with the new planetary wisdom born in the United Nations. When I was a young UN official, my superiors usually suppressed the word "world" in my writings, replacing it by "international." Today, the words most often used at the UN are: the planet, the globe, interdependent, planetary, global. The human mind has expanded its vision considerably. And yet, the words: universe, cosmic, God, Creation, infinity, eternity, soul, and spirituality are still missing in the world organization.

Humanity must concentrate again on the definition of God, of what His will is likely to be for our planet and life in the vast universe and colossal stream of time. Only then will we find the ways of right human behavior and of making this planet a haven of peace, beauty, justice, and happiness. We must reestablish the reign of God on Earth. We must think, feel, and act like universal beings. We must find the rules and laws of the universe as they apply to our planet. We must strive to become the most perfect planet in Creation, the Planet of God. This is what is really expected of us.

From a reader:

"Your work on global spirituality and research into the mystical experience seem to be among the only ways available to counteract the self-destructive tendencies of humankind. The essential unity of humankind *will be* experienced either through the simultaneous death of most of us in a nuclear inferno, or through the rising into the consciousness of billions of us of a religious, mystical vision of the unity of the human family."

Each individual, each institution, each entity, and each human group must ask itself this question: What can I contribute to a better world and to a happy human family? Then there will be unity of purpose, unity in diversity. Then there will be peace on Earth.

See the world with global eyes.
Love the world with a global heart.
Understand the world with a global mind.
Merge with the world through a global spirit.

If we would ask God about the future of our planet, He would answer: "It is in your hands."

The great blessing by Dame Fate was
to place me at the center of world affairs
whence I could observe humanity and the globe
at the precise moment when the human race was
    becoming one,
the world global, nations interdependent, the people
knowledgeable of one another,
and our planet visible from outer space as a self-
    contained
tiny spaceship in the universe.

THE UNITED NATIONS

Someday humans will understand that the United
Nations is a great biological breakthrough, an evolutionary turning point for the world and the universe.

If you want to find the true agenda of humanity, turn
to the UN and to its specialized agencies and you will
find it. These new world agencies are indeed the biological indicators of our current and future evolutionary yearnings.

What I like about the UN is that it seldom ponders over old ground and instead concentrates on the present and the future. The new, interdependent world which is in the making has no precedent. Looking at the past cannot be of any great help, except to study our mistakes. An eleven year old girl wrote to me: "Regarding our place in time, I think that we should learn what our mistakes were in the past, fix our mistakes in the present, and make the future better."

The beauty, culture and sharing of hearts and minds that occurs in the United Nations on a day-to-day basis is astounding and should never be measured on the yardstick of instantaneous results, as some would want.

Margaret Mead used to say to her students: "Go and study the United Nations, which is for the anthropologists of today what New Guinea was during my youth."

As meteorologists warn people of impending
   weather dangers,
so the UN warns humanity of impending global
   dangers.

This deeply revealing prayer of a doctor to his
   patient:
"Please help me to save you."
This same prayer of the United Nations to
   humanity:
"Please help me to save you."

The United Nations must become the world's supreme moral institution.

Like any simple peasant I have put all my love and care into a plot of earth; on my plot stands the rectangle of the United Nations along the river of the rising sun in New York.

In our dream of a perfect planet, there are no wars, no violence, no hatred, no injustices, no drugs, no alcohol, no armaments, no nuclear dangers, no fouled air, water, and soils. All these dreams converge for the first time ever on a universal scale in the United Nations. So do their obstacles and birthpains. What I cannot understand is why people are not more supportive of the United Nations and why the children of this planet are not better educated about it.

The UN is the greatest human service organization on Earth, and by being that it is an instrument of God. To work for the UN is a true ministry.

The world is in search of a new ideology, spirituality or vision for the future. Its most notable manifestations are: the effort of Catholicism to integrate justice in its universal spirituality; the development of a spiritual civilization by the Chinese, through the integration of science, materialism and justice into Confucian harmonies; the transcendence of Japanese scientific and economic success into Buddhism; India's return to a cosmic view of all earthly and human phenomena; the New Age movements of the United States; and the vision of harmonies emerging from the United Nations: harmony with our planetary home, harmony between all human groups, harmony with the past and the future, harmony with the universe, individual harmony and fulfillment as the ultimate objective of all our efforts.

The UN is not disappointing, but endlessly exciting. After 36 years of service with it, I am more enthusiastic than ever about its potential role for the successful evolution of the human race. So help me God.

At the age of twenty, when I came out of World War II, I was a very disillusioned, pessimistic young man who thought that within twenty years there would be another world war. Today, at the age of sixty, after so many years at the center of world affairs, I am ready to bet for the success of the human species which will fulfill the expectations of God.

"Working at the edge of the development of human society is to work on the brink of the unknown. Much of what is done will one day prove to have been of little avail. That is no excuse for the failure to act in accordance with our best understanding, in recognition of its limits but with faith in the ultimate result of the creative evolution in which it is our privilege to cooperate".

Dag Hammarskjöld

Dear reader, with your hearty participation and cooperation, we will succeed. My advice is this:

Decide to network
Use every letter you write
Every conversation you have
Every meeting you attend
To express your fundamental beliefs and dreams
Affirm to others the vision of the world you want
Network through thought
Network through action
Network through love
Network through the spirit
You are the center of a network
You are the center of the world
You are a free, immensely powerful source
of life and goodness
Affirm it
Spread it
Radiate it
Think day and night about it
And you will see a miracle happen:
the greatness of your own life.
In a world of big powers, media, and monopolies
But of four and a half billion individuals
Networking is the new freedom
the new democracy
a new form of happiness.

Robert Muller

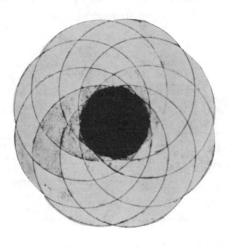